MW00873378

Smart Marketing
For Tutors

A Step-by-Step Guide To Building Your Online Tutoring Business Using Free Marketing Tools

7 STEPS TO

GETTING STARTED

AS AN ONLINE TUTOR

FOR ASPIRING AND EXPERIENCED TUTORS

DOWNLOAD YOUR COPY

Click here to get your copy: http://eepurl.com/KFlD9

Introduction

The tutoring industry is one of the fastest growing industries in the world. Furthermore, research shows that it is at present a $5 billion dollar market and an industry that is set to see exponential growth over the next few years. If you're someone who has ever thought about tutoring but have no idea where to start with marketing your services then this book is for you.

If you're thinking about starting a tutoring or education-related business like an education consultancy then it's in your best interest to keep reading. As an experienced tutor and someone that has tutored for several years, the advice I'm giving is based on both research and personal experience. Unlike other books out there that focus on "theories" about marketing your tutoring business, this book is based on tried and tested methods that actually attract high quality clients.

These are the exact methods I've used to grow and build my tutoring business and they don't just apply to tutors who live in a specific country or city, they apply to tutors who live anywhere. Furthermore, the advice is especially suited to tutors who want to teach online and build their online tutoring business. Nonetheless, you can also use these strategies to build your local or offline tutoring business.

What really inspired me to write this book was my experience of receiving thousands of emails from my newsletter subscribers. Many of them had fears about how to start their tutoring business when they had no money, how to attract clients without wasting money on advertising and how to know which advertising or marketing channels worked. The idea of wasting precious time testing different (and often expensive) methods frightened them and I could understand why. I started my tutoring business when I had very little money and no contacts or connections in the education industry. It took a lot of trial and error before I managed to find marketing methods that worked for me and required no upfront costs. I studied and digested everything there was to know about digital marketing, social media marketing and optimizing websites. In essence, it's taken me years to learn all of these things but it doesn't need to take you anywhere near that length of time if you simply follow the steps I've outlined in this book.

If you're looking for an in-depth book that covers offline marketing strategies take a look at my other book 'Become A Private Tutor' which is available to purchase on Amazon. More importantly, make sure you download my free 7 step guide on online tutoring here: http://eepurl.com/KFlD9.

Why do you want to tutor?

In recent years, tutoring has become a popular career choice for a variety of people. From slick city lawyers who teach in their spare time to university students who teach to make a few extra dollars a day, it's a profession that appeals to almost anybody that has a knack for teaching.

However, many people who enter the tutoring profession simply because it's 'cool' or 'trendy' usually don't last as tutors. Those who last in this line of work are the people who are dedicated, committed and education-passionate. The majority of 'successful' tutors are those who deeply care about teaching, sharing their knowledge with the world and bettering the lives of their students. Put simply, if you're going to become a tutor or want a long-lasting tutoring career then you should be someone who genuinely cares about teaching and have a knack for it.

In my book, Become a Private Tutor, I discuss the key marks of a great tutor. In essence, great tutors are people who love teaching, are patient enough to understand that everybody learns at a different pace and care about delivering an outstanding service. Are you willing to do these things on a consistent basis? Are you willing to go above and beyond to your clients and students? Do you have the ability to really give this profession your all? Yes? Then read on!

Before we dive into the marketing strategies that smart tutors use, I want you to be clear on where you are on your journey. Have you briefly thought about tutoring but haven't gone into great depth to figure out what it is you want to teach? Are you in contrast an experienced tutor who has been teaching for years but is stuck with how to get new clients or scale your business? Are you a parent that has hired tutors in the past but longs to take it up yourself because you know you have what it takes? Or are you in a completely different position? Before we move into the next section I want you to write down a one-sentence summary that describes where you are now on this journey.

What is marketing and how is it different for tutors?

Often we hear the words marketing and advertising interchangeably used. However, they are different. Marketing essentially refers to free or low cost methods that are used to promote your business to your target market. In comparison, advertising refers to promoting your business using paid channels and mechanisms such as newspaper, magazine or television ads.

When people usually start a tutoring business, they often start with an initial excitement and eagerness, which is perfectly natural. They then do a bit of research and realise that whilst teaching isn't in itself expensive to do, promoting your services as a tutor can be. Naturally, many people who are new to the industry opt to promote themselves by advertising their services on expensive platforms or publications. This might seem like a logical and perfectly normal choice but it is also expensive. Adverts can cost thousands and don't always lead to new clients or any form of financial return. Furthermore, tutors who have success with media adverts are usually fairly experienced and are able to negotiate good rates or simply have the experience needed to create advertising campaigns that are persuasive and generate new clientele. In contrast, someone who is new to tutoring is unlikely to be able to get the same results with a costly ad.

This isn't to put you off or to suggest that media adverts aren't a worthwhile form of advertising. Adverts of all forms can be a great way to promote your tutoring services. However, this book will explicitly deal with free or low-cost online marketing channels that will help you to promote your business without paying thousands or even hundreds to do so. The problem that most tutors face is that they want to attract high quality clients and generate new leads without spending a fortune and that's exactly what I'll teach you to do. Still reading? Let's move on.

Why forward-thinking tutors win

Now you've hopefully clarified where you are on your journey and you've discovered that paid advertising methods aren't necessarily the best, it's time to look at the benefits of online advertising as well as the importance of being a forward-thinking tutor.

Traditionally, a student would study at home and a tutor would come to their house to teach them a particular subject. This method of learning dates back hundreds of years. Traditional one-to-one, face-to-face tutoring has been the norm for centuries. However, with the advent of the internet, the tutoring industry has changed and many students now learn online. They simply select a tutor and learn a particular subject via Skype, WizIQ, Google+ etc. There are literally dozens of platforms that make virtual learning a breeze. When I encourage my clients to teach online, many of them are aspiring tutors, they're often reluctant to try online tutoring and just want to focus on teaching students on a face-to-face basis. Although, I love tutoring in the traditional format, the reality is that if you want to expand your business's potential for finding clients and help more people, it's crucial that you are at least open to teaching online. You don't need to spend hours researching online tutoring or become a guru at Skype teaching, you simply need to be open to accepting requests that come from students who live in other states, cities or countries and want online lessons.

Before we delve into how to find clients, I'm going to outline some of the benefits of online tutoring.

- It saves your clients time because they don't need to spend hours travelling to you.
- It saves you time because you don't need to travel to students or make arrangements for finding a suitable venue to teach in.
- It saves your clients money because there are no additional costs required to hire you. For example, they don't need to pay for your transportation fees. This means that you can widen and increase your client base

because more people can afford your services and you're therefore more likely to receive enquiries and bookings.
- It allows you to teach from the comfort of your own home.
- You can teach students from a variety of backgrounds and cultures.
- You can widen your social network by establishing rapport with clients from across the globe.
- You only need a web cam, computer (or laptop) to get started.

There are several more advantages but the ones above should be enough to give you an idea of how effective online tutoring can be.

Now that you've not only learnt about the importance of being open-minded and open-hearted, it's time to delve into the marketing tools that smart tutors use to get high quality clients and generate new leads.

Facebook Marketing

To market your tutoring business on Facebook, the first thing you need is a personal Facebook profile. To set one up is easy, just head over to Facebook.com and sign up for a free account.

Once you have an account, fill it in by adding a few basic details about yourself and add a photo. If you don't have a photo people will assume you're a spanner and it will be difficult to reach out to fellow business owners who can support and promote your business.

Once that's sorted. Head over to the button that says 'create a page' and follow the instructions for creating a local business page.

The option to create a page will be on the left hand column underneath your name and messages/events buttons.

You should see this on the left-hand side of the page:

Once you click the 'create page' button you should see this:

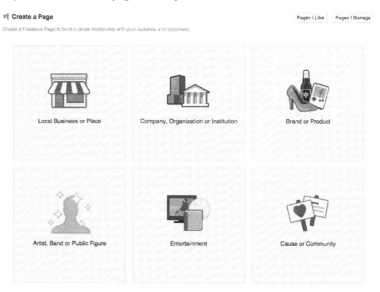

Click on the 'local business or place button' and you'll then be able to create your business page.

Your business page should ideally be named after your business and should include the primary subject that you teach. For example, Victoria's Spanish Tutoring Service.

If you have a clever or witty name, you can of course use that instead. For example, one of my favourite business Facebook pages is called Grammar Girl. The name is catchy, short and gives us an idea of what sort of business the owner runs.

After choosing a name for your business and Facebook profile, you should then begin adding photos of yourself teaching or interesting photos that relate to education, educational development or the specific subject you teach.

Here are some examples of good profiles from education and tutoring companies:

Kumon UK:

Like · Comment · Share   ↗ 14 Shares

👍 19 people like this.

Write a comment...

Kumon UK
October 24

Let's end the week with some fun Friday trivia:
John Steinbeck's original manuscript for 'Of Mice and Men' (which features on the Kumon Recommended Reading List) was eaten by his dog!

Steinbeck wrote to his agent following the incident, saying: "I was pretty mad, but the poor little fellow may have been acting critically."
http://www.kumon-english-ri.com/

POSTS TO PAGE   >

Katie Deans
October 4 at 11:20pm

Anyone know where I can get / buy Kumon achievement KIS medals? I ha.... See More

Like · Comment

Jules Glandfield
September 30 at 8:16pm

Hi is Kumon suitable for Dyslexic children ?

Like · Comment   💬 2

National Literacy Trust
September 19 at 12:08pm

💬 Video celebrating Books about Town. Own an iconic piece of literary history at auction on Oct 7

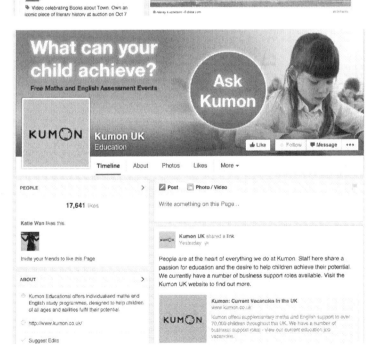

What can your child achieve?
Free Maths and English Assessment Events

Ask Kumon

KUMON | **Kumon UK**
Education

👍 Like   + Follow   💬 Message   •••

Timeline   About   Photos   Likes   More ▾

PEOPLE   >

17,641 likes

Katie Wan likes this.

Invite your friends to like this Page

ABOUT   >

Kumon Educational offers individualised maths and English study programmes, designed to help children of all ages and abilities fulfil their potential.

http://www.kumon.co.uk/

✓ Suggest Edits

✏ Post   🖼 Photo / Video

Write something on this Page...

Kumon UK shared a link
Yesterday

People are at the heart of everything we do at Kumon. Staff here share a passion for education and the desire to help children achieve their potential. We currently have a number of business support roles available. Visit the Kumon UK website to find out more.

KUMON

Kumon: Current Vacancies in the UK
www.kumon.co.uk

Kumon offers supplementary maths and English support to over 70,000 children throughout the UK. We have a number of business support roles - view our current education job vacancies.

Grammar Girl (her page is amazing!)

Science Sparks

I love Grammar Girl's page in particular because it tells you what she does (she teaches grammar), she has niched down and doesn't just teach 'English' but a specific area of English and she's also created a brand (which is something that all tutors should aspire to create).

Spend some time looking for great education and tutoring profiles on Facebook and use those as inspiration for your own.

If you'd like to get gorgeous graphics created (like Grammar Girl did) check out fiverr.com and odesk.com and search for 'graphic designers' who can create images and graphics for your business within a few days.

Also click the 'about' section of your profile to fill in details such as your website address (url), your phone number, email and blog page.

About		Basic Info	
Creative science fun for everyone! http://www.science-sparks.com/		Joined Facebook	07/03/2011
Description			
Education blog full of fun and exciting science activities for kids.		Release Date	July 30, 2011
http://www.science-sparks.com/ http://www.pinterest.com/sciencesparks		Awards	MAD Blog Award winner 2012
		Contact Info	
		Email	sciencesparks1@gmail.com
		Website	http://www.science-sparks.com

If you don't have a website (yet) simply fill this section in with your contact number and email. In the **description box** mention that you're able to tutor students and welcome people to get in touch with you. You can also briefly mention your experience and tell potential clients a little bit about yourself.

How To Increase The number of Facebook Fans You Have:

#1. Post Great Content

Read online publications like The Guardian & The Huffington Post and every time you spot an article that relates to education, share it on your Facebook page. Your fans will love you for it and you'll attract more 'likers' or fans.
These fans can very easily turn into customers so give them the best content by updating your Facebook page regularly and posting to it on a frequent basis.

#2 Ask Questions

You can also ask them questions like:
"How's your day going?"
'What do you struggle with at school?"
"What do you like/dislike about (the subject you teach?

The more engaged you are with them, the more they'll grow to like you and will in turn book you for tutoring lessons.

How To Market On Facebook Like A Boss!

The BEST way to promote your Facebook page is to join private '**groups**' in Facebook.

Groups are like communities within Facebook and there are hundreds (possibly thousands) of them. Use the search box in Facebook to find groups that relate to both what you teach and your target market.

The ultimate goal is to find out where your target market are and join groups that are filled with them.

And by target market, I'm not necessarily talking about students or children.

For instance, I teach children aged 7-11 but my target market when promoting my business is not children. It's actually their parents because their parents are the ones who'll pay me to teach.

Remember, your target client is always the person who pays you to teach. It's not a teenager or child but a paying adult.

So, to find their parents, I've joined dozens of Facebook groups that are filled with mums who live in and around my area.

I went onto Facebook and searched for 'London Mums,' 'Stay at home mums' etc.

Think about the sort of groups your target market might be a part of and start joining those groups.

For example, if you teach Maths to children under 16, join groups for mums that are education focused or do a search for 'strict mums' or 'Maths mums' and see what you find.

The key is to look for groups where your target market will be.

Step by step instructions

1. Login to Facebook
2. In the search button type in words related to your target market
Example:

3. Scroll down to where it says 'see more results.' Then click the 'GROUPS' button and Facebook will show you a list of groups that are relevant.

For example:

Once you've found a group, click the '**join group**' button and that will tell the administrator of the group to add you. After a few days or so, you should be a member of the group.

You'll need to **join about 5 groups** that each have roughly 300+ members in order to get good results.

So how do you make these groups a marketing channel for your business?

Whenever you post something onto your business Facebook page, click the **SHARE** button (at the bottom of the post) and then click the button that lets you share the post with a specific group.

See the screenshots below:

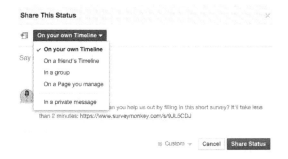

Here's an example of what your 'share' will look like:

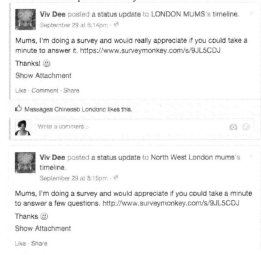

Sharing your posts with groups is the quickest way to grow the number of Facebook fans you have and it's absolutely free.

The reason why it allows you to grow your Facebook fan numbers is because your post will now be seen by the people who are members of these groups and the members will often click on your post and LIKE your Facebook page. Members of groups are usually very involved in the group communities and will read anything that's posted there.

Make sure that you encourage people to not only read your post but to head over to your Facebook page to LIKE it.

For example, my friend Brandon does a great job of this when he shares his posts in relevant groups on Facebook:

Stone leftover from another project and three galvanized trash can lids become a bird bath grouping! Another of my "use what you have" ventures.

Share with your home & garden friends!
LIKE Easy Garden Bag for more daily Home & Garden fun!

Brandon's business is in the gardening field so whenever he shares one of his Facebook posts on a group page, he adds the phrase 'LIKE Easy Garden Bag for more daily Home & Garden fun!'

You could do something similar and add a phrase such as 'LIKE Victoria's Tutoring service for more parenting tips.'

I use this method all the time on one of my other Facebook pages (not The Tutoress) and it actually helped me to gain hundreds of new Facebook fans within a few days.

I then went on to promote things to those new fans which is exactly what you can do.

Your homework:
- Create a Facebook Business Page
- Add photos and posts to it
- Post good regular content (this can come from other websites like The Guardian's education section or from your own blog- if you have one)
- Find at least 5 groups (where your target market hang out)
- Join those groups
- Share your Facebook posts by clicking the SHARE button that's underneath each post.
- Repeat this process every few days and watch your Facebook LIKES grow!

Bonus homework: after your Facebook LIKES start to grow, post links from your own website or blog.

The key is that you have to be consistent with posting on Facebook and promoting your page in the groups if you want to see results.

The alternative is Facebook advertising but that's complicated to set up and it costs quite a bit.

Resources that rock!
Here are my favourite resources on Facebook marketing

12 Days To Facebook Fame by the incredible Brandon Wagner:
https://soundcloud.com/bethedove/12-days-of-facebook-my-step-by

His advice in this recording totally changed how I used Facebook.

Social Media Marketing Podcast
https://soundcloud.com/social_media_marketing

LKR Social Media
http://www.lkrsocialmedia.com/blog
Also check out Laura's social media pages as they're great examples of how to
turn your social media marketing into money. https://twitter.com/lkr and
http://www.facebook.com/lkrsocialmedia

I'll be sharing more great resources with my newsletter subscribers; click here to
sign up or visit www.thetutoress.com/resources.

Twitter Marketing

To market your tutoring business on Twitter, the first thing you need is a Twitter profile which will be used solely for business purposes. To set one up is easy, just head over to Twitter.com and sign up for a free account.

Once you have an account, you need to give yourself a Twitter page name.

The name of your tutoring business would be best to use.
For instance, my business is called The Tutoress so my Twitter name is @The Tutoress.

Fill in your profile by adding photos and a brief description about your tutoring business.

Twitter is all about short and quick social media interactions so they limit the amount of words you can use to describe yourself to about 140 characters or so.

Once you've created a name, added a photo and filled in your description, you can play around with Twitter by posting a few tweets.

The tweets on your Twitter page can consist of the following:

Updates related to your business e.g. are you looking for new students this month? Are you looking for promotional partners who work in the education sector?

Post these things by asking questions or simply posting notifications about what's happening in your business.

Ask a question that your target market might be thinking about. For instance, you could post something like this:
'Got SATs exams this week? Tell me, do you feel prepared or petrified? '
'What do you dislike about Math the most and why?'

Asking questions is a great way to interact with your followers.

The Tutoress @TheTutoress · Sep 27

#Parents, can you help us out by filling in this short survey? It'll take less than 3 minutes: surveymonkey.com/s/9JL5CDJ #Mumsnet #mums #dads

1   1

The Tutoress @TheTutoress · Oct 24

Mums, who are your favourite parenting/mummy bloggers? #mums #moms #mompreneur

You can also ask questions that promote your services like:
'Do you need a Spanish tutor? Tweet me to book a 15 minute trial online lesson- it'll be so fun!'

Twitter is quite a relaxed social media platform so make sure your tweets are casual in tone. There's no need to write like a journalist. Tweet as if you're talking to your big brother/sister and keep your tone of writing **classy yet casual**.

Another brilliant way of using **Twitter is to post links to your own articles, blog posts or web pages**. Google will actually give your website a thumbs up each time you do this!

The Tutoress @TheTutoress · Oct 11

Just found out that 3 of our students passed the QE Boys exam! We're hoping for a 100% success rate this year! bit.ly/1mKCPDf

1

Google loves it when your site is being mentioned in the social media stratosphere so try to post at least one tweet a week that links back to your website.

You can also keep your followers engaged by posting links from other websites (that are not owned by tutors in the same market).
For example, I sometimes tweet articles from BBC News:

Avamind @Avamind · Sep 25

BBC News - Poor parent-child bonding 'hampers learning' bbc.com/news/education...

4

To find potential clients on Twitter you can do two things:

Find companies/individuals that run businesses that are not in direct competition with yours but are somewhat aligned with your business.

For instance, I recently received a tweet from a company that provides after school music tuition.

They're not direct competitors but we both have the same market in mind-parents of children who live in London or in the UK.

Because I'm now connected to them through Twitter, this gives me the option of discussing a potential collaboration with them or asking them whether they'd like to promote my courses or lessons in exchange for a referral fee.

I could also promote their services to my clients and receive a commission for doing so.

Since using Twitter I've created connections and partnerships with various education companies that are not direct competitors but target similar (or the same) clients as I do.

When you reach out to fellow tutors/education companies, make sure your tweet is friendly and professional. Say hi and try to build a relationship with each tutor/company over time.

You can also 'retweet' or 'favourite' their tweets as a way of gently making yourself known to them.
After a bit of interaction with the tutor/company on twitter, ask for their email address and then send them a polite email and mention that you spoke with them on twitter and want to discuss the possibility of collaborating with them.

The second way of using Twitter to find clients is to search for parents, students and adult learners using Twitter's search box.

Simply enter a word or phrase that describes your target market and look through the list of suggestions to find potential clients. For instance, if you're a tutor who's target market are parents that live in Florida then you could type in 'Florida mum' and see who comes up.

You can then follow the people who come up, read their profiles and tweets and then send a friendly tweet to them or reply to one of their tweets.

The thing with Twitter is that about 25% of the people who you follow will follow you back so bear that in mind as you begin following people. If you follow 100 and 25 follow back, you can simply unfollow the remaining 75 people and then continue searching for new potential clients to follow.

You can use a free service like https://www.just**unfollow**.com which will tell you which of your followers are not following back and it will allow you to unfollow them quickly and easily.

By the way, if you have no idea what a hashtag (#) is, it's simply a symbol that's used on Twitter and a few other social media platforms that allows people to find posts and comments that are related to certain topics.

Essentially, each hashtag represents a topic or phrase that people are talking about. When you use the hashtag it makes it easy for people tweets that are related to a particular topic. For instance, if you use the hashtag #drinks in one of your tweets then anyone who searches Twitter for #drinks will find your tweet.

Tutors can use hashtags like #tutors #tutoring #tutorneeded #tutorswanted #teacherswanted #teachers #edchat #parents #englishlessons #mathslessons #maths #moms and #dads to make their tweets findable and by using such hashtags people that are looking for tweets or information related to these topics will find you.

I try to use at least one hashtag in each of my tweets so that potential clients can find me.

The third way of using Twitter to attract clients is to contact journalists and media outlets that are on the hunt for stories relating to education. If you do a search for #educationnews, #reporterrequest or #journalistrequest you're likely to find journalists that are looking for stories. You can also use the hashtag #HARO to find requests from Help A Reporter Out.

Getting featured in media outlets, local and national magazines and newspapers can do wonders for your tutoring business so dedicate some time (like 30 minutes a week) to PR.

This can be in the form of replying to journalist's tweets, using Twitter to find journalists information or replying to requests that you find through services like HARO (which stands for Help A Reporter Out).

Finding journalist's email addresses can be quite difficult but one of the great things about Twitter is that it makes it a lot easier to track journalists down and to introduce yourself to them in a casual and non-pushy sort of way.

For instance, if I was looking for a journalist for a parenting magazine, I'd type something like 'editor parenting magazine' into Twitter and I'd see who'd come up. I'd then start following those people and gradually building a relationship with them.

When I searched for 'editor parenting magazine' I discovered dozens of potential contacts.

Remember that Twitter is all about **making personal interactions** and communicating in a way that's **casual yet classy**. Don't be spammy or pushy.

You should of course use your Twitter page to promote your services but try to still with the 60-40 principle. 60% of your posts should be light and conversational and 40% should be promotional (but not spammy).

Your homework:
- Create a Twitter Page or update your existing one.
- Add photos and posts to your page
- Post good regular content (this can come from your website and other websites like BBC news or BBC education)
- Post 1 promotional tweet this week.
- Retweet or favourite one post from a potential client.

Bonus homework: follow 100 new potential clients on Twitter and after 7 days see who's followed you back. Unfollow those who don't follow back and then write down how many new followers you gained during the 7-day period.

Resources that rock
Here are my favourite resources on Facebook marketing

ProBlogger
http://www.problogger.net/archives/2011/04/15/how-a-few-tweets-led-to-a-370-increase-in-my-traffic/

Social Media Etiquette by Chris Brogan
http://chrisbrogan.com/socialmediaetiquette/

How To Thank Someone For A Retweet
http://www.convinceandconvert.com/social-media-tools/7-ways-to-thank-someone-for-a-retwee/

Powerful Twitter Marketing Rules
http://www.jeffbullas.com/2014/01/24/11-essential-rules-for-powerful-twitter-marketing/

LinkedIn Marketing

LinkedIn, for those who don't know, is a social media platform for professionals.

It's a great site for tutors to use because it's relatively easy to find your potential client there.

For instance, if you're an English Tutor who teaches adults how to speak English, you can simply join groups for EFL (English as a Foreign Language) learners. If you teach Latin you could search for groups for Latin-enthusiasts or Harry Potter Fans that want to learn Latin. The options are endless!

To get started with LinkedIn, head over to www.linkedin.com and sign up for a free account.

Yes, LinkedIn is free but there are paid options for people who want to take advantage of its more advanced features.

From my experience, I don't think it's necessary to sign up for a paid account. A free account will usually take you quite far.

Once you've signed up for an account, begin filling it in with your professional details, qualifications and make sure you add a photo. Profiles with photos tend to come across as being spammy so a photo is essential.

Ideally, you should have a professional headshot photo of yourself. If you don't have one simply ask a friend to take a photo of your face. Your photo should look smart and represent you in the best light possible.

Here are some examples of headshot photos:

Underneath your name, you'll see an area called 'your title.' Your title describes what you do for a living and to get better results from LinkedIn it's important to make sure that your title mentions your tutoring business or the fact that you're a tutor.

Even if you're just getting started it's important to include the word tutor in your title.

Here's an example of mine:

Vicky Olubi
Award-Winning Entrepreneur, Author & 11+ Tutor.
London, United Kingdom | Education Management

Current   My Curls, TheTutoress.com
Education   B-School

You can see that my title includes the phrase '11+ tutor.'
This tells people that I specialize in teaching the 11+ (a popular exam in the UK).

Your profile title might say something like 'Latin Tutor New York' or 'Chemistry Tutor London.' If you teach online it might say 'International Online Chemistry Tutor.'

Once you've completed your profile, added a great headshot photo and have a brilliant title, it's now time to start networking on LinkedIn.

Try to make sure that most of your contacts are potential clients or people that could help you to promote your tutoring business in exchange for you promoting their services/products to the people you know.

There are 2 types of connections you need to make:

- Individuals who run businesses or work for companies that might want to promote your services in exchange for you promoting theirs.

- Groups that contain parents (if you teach children or teenagers) or potential students or clients that fit your target market.

To find individuals who run companies, type in words that relate to the sort of people you're looking for.

For instance, if you teach Geography to High School students, search for 'geography games' or 'geography apps' or 'geography specialist' etc. The goal is to find individuals/companies that you can work with over time and these people will refer clients your way.

Your task:
- Who will you search for when you're using LinkedIn?
- Think of 3 individuals/companies and enter phrases or search terms into LinkedIn.

- Add those 3 people as connections and when adding them, send them a little message introducing yourself. Keep it friendly and classy.

As with anything, it's about consistency so make sure you schedule some time in your calendar to use LinkedIn to build your connections, network and reach out to potential clients or promotional partners.

Ideally, you should spend a total of 30 minutes a week on social media marketing. Once you get the hang of it, it doesn't take long to add a few connections each week and send a few messages to potential promotional partners.

Now that you've learnt to add individuals or companies, it's time to leverage the power of groups.

Groups in LinkedIn are similar to those on Facebook.

They're mini-communities within the larger community of LinkedIn.

These groups often contain hundreds or even thousands of people that are passionate about a particular topic. Essentially, the people who join groups are usually proactive people and they're always on the lookout for the best 'thing' within that particular group or community.

How To Use LinkedIn Groups

1. Think about who your target client is.

If you teach children then your target client is their parent and it's most likely to be a mother. If it's an adult learner then you simply have to look for groups that adult learners might be a part of.

2. Using the search box, type in some words related to the type of group your ideal client might be a member of. For instance, if I were a Math Tutor who taught High School students then I'd look for groups that were for mothers in my town, city or area. For example, I might type in "London mums."

Here's what a quick search revealed:

Another tip is to search for 'parents' and click 'Groups' (on your left) and then see which groups come up.

Here's an example:

Similarly, if I knew that my target client was a professional mother then I might look for groups for professional mums etc.

3. Once you find a group, request to join it and once you've been approved become an active part of each group community.

To get involved you can do the following:

- Ask questions
- Answer questions or concerns people have
- Make comments on posts
- Mention your tutoring services on occasion but chances are that people will click on your profile to learn more about what you do once they see you interacting in the group. They can then contact you if they need to ask a question about your services.

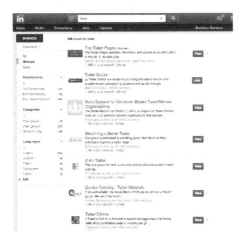

4. Spend a few minutes each week replying to posts, sharing things that are relevant and subtly mentioning your tutoring business.

Don't spam the group; just casually mention something related to your business when necessary. Another great thing to do is to look for groups for tutors and join them.

You might be doubtful about whether LinkedIn could work for your tutoring business but being a part of various LinkedIn groups has helped me to:

- Get featured in national media outlets which gave my business a lot of exposure.
- Attracted the attention of potential investors (which was totally unexpected!)
- Attracted high-quality clients.
- Helped me to form partnerships with companies and individuals who promote my business FOR me.

All of the above things came as a result of simply getting involved in LinkedIn groups.

I spend about 10 minutes a week getting involved and it's definitely worthwhile doing the same.

Your homework:

- Join LinkedIn and fill in your profile.
- Search for individuals and companies that could make great promotional partners.
- Add individuals as 'connections' and send a brief 'hello' message introducing yourself and what you do.
- Search for groups that contain potential clients like mum groups, parenting groups, foreign language groups, international student groups and university groups.
- Join at least 3 and start getting involved in the groups.
- Subtly mention your tutoring business and how you help people (only when it's relevant to the post).
- Spend about 10 minutes each week on LinkedIn marketing and a total of 30 minutes each week on social media marketing.

LinkedIn Resources That Rock!

Here are my favourite resources on LinkedIn marketing:

Social Media Examiner
http://www.socialmediaexaminer.com/tag/linkedin-marketing/

http://www.socialmediaexaminer.com/finding-clients-on-linkedin/

Make Social Media Sell
http://www.makesocialmediasell.com/how-to-use-linkedin-to-find-clients/

DIY Themes
http://diythemes.com/thesis/linkedin-marketing/

Lewis Howes
http://lewishowes.com/linkedin/linkedin-business-marketing-tips/

Positioning Yourself As A High-Paid Tutor Through PR

PR – whether it is on the local radio, in online magazines or on blogs can do wonders for your tutoring business.

PR (which means Public Relations) can get your business in front of the very people that desire and need your services the most. It can also help to establish you as being a brilliant tutor because it's a form of third-party endorsement.

The fact of the matter is that people trust media publications and when they feature a business owner or expert, people assume that person is great at what they do.

Take for instance, Gordon Ramsey. He's the British guy that shouts and swears a lot. For all we know he could be the worst chef on the planet but the fact that he's on the cover of magazines, on TV and has his own cookbooks makes the public see him as being a culinary expert. If he commanded $1,000 per minute for a cooking lesson, dozens of people would pay for it and that's simply because he's a public figure and he's not afraid of putting himself out there in order to promote his books and restaurants. Fair enough, not all of his PR has been positive but for the most part he's established a world-renowned reputation as being one of the world's top chefs. But is he really or has he just positioned himself (through PR) as being great?

People place a greater level of trust on those that have been featured positively in the media. That means that as a tutor it's important that if you want to attract good quality clients (that don't haggle or drive you nuts) you ought to get at least some positive PR.

PR can take the shape of various forms but here are some examples of the kinds of PR you should consider.

Local magazines

Local newspapers

International magazines

International magazines and newspapers are great if you teach online and just because they're international that doesn't mean you can't reach out to them to suggest a potential story idea. So far as that story relates to their readers then it's likely to be of interest to them. For instance, I teach online and most of my students are from the United Arab Emirates, I could therefore reach out to a few of their magazines/newspapers to suggest that they write an article on the popularity of online tutors amongst Middle-Eastern parents. They could then interview me and I could talk a bit about my business and how it relates to the story.

If you're considering tutoring online then reaching out to international publications is a great way to get yourself in front of potential international clients.

Examples:

If you're emailing journalists make sure you put your business's web address or name beside your own name.

For example, Victoria (Founder of TheTutoress.com)

I recently had a journalist contact me and he knew me as "The Tutoress" which means that when I'm featured in his publication they're more likely to mention my site. That could essentially bring me great PR, new enquiries and new clients.

Teaching/Education/ Parenting publications

Whether you teach dance, music, English or Math, there are dozens of specialist magazines for teachers, parents and tutors. Head over to Google and type in the name of the subject you teach and the word 'magazine' and you should find a few publications.

Start researching these magazines (most information is available on their websites) and find the name and email address of their Features Editor.

Being featured in specialist magazines, radio shows and newspapers can open up doors for your tutoring business and will position you as one of the best tutors in your field.

You can also create a *PRESS* page or *As Seen In* section on your website and list the various magazines/newspapers/radio shows that you've been featured in.

For example:

Create an "As Seen In" box with logos of media outlets where you've appeared
Photo courtesy of www.clientaltraction.com

One of the benefits of having an 'As Seen In' or 'As Featured In' section on your website is that it instantly makes people think that your business has been featured in trustworthy publications. This makes potential clients feel more comfortable about choosing you because they automatically assume that you're a trustworthy and highly regarded tutor.

It also aligns you with the publications you've been featured in and makes potential clients take you more seriously. For instance, the lady pictured above has aligned herself with Forbes and Inc. by placing their logos in the 'As Seen' section of her website.

If your business gets featured or mentioned in any media outlet, blog or newspaper, don't be afraid to add their logo to the 'As Seen' section of your website. However, make sure you have permission from the company before using their logo and also only do this if you have genuinely been featured.

Online parenting and education magazines/blogs are another great outlet for getting PR mentions. Some examples of such publications are below.

If you teach children under the age of about 15 then being quoted or featured in a parenting magazine is a great way to reach new potential clients and they'll gladly pay more for your services because they see you as being an education expert. After all, who doesn't want the best tutor teaching their child?

To start with, it's best to target local ones and then move onto national ones.

To find local parenting magazines simply Google 'your area + parenting magazine.' Head over to their websites and look in the 'contact us' areas for contact details of their journalists/writers/editors.

It's worth introducing yourself to their writers and simply letting them know that you'd be happy to contribute your expert opinions to any parenting, teaching or education-related articles that they are writing. You can also suggest potential ideas to them. For instance, if there's a hot topic in the education field, you can offer to discuss it with them or share tips on how to tackle it.

In terms of parenting/education/homeschooling blogs, there are again hundreds (perhaps thousands) of them out there but it can help if you start with getting featured in local ones first and then gradually reaching out to local and even international ones.

Examples:
http://www.confessionsofahomeschooler.com/
http://www.gsheller.com/
http://www.confessionsofahomeschooler.com/

If you find a good, local parenting blog, it's worth asking the owner if they'd like to interview you about the subject you teach and how your work helps local parents/children/students.

What do you do after you've received a PR feature?

- Getting PR can bring some amazing opportunities (and clients) your way but it's important to 'show off' your PR features by doing the following:
- Mentioning them on Twitter a few times and let your followers know that you're excited to have been featured somewhere!
- Tweet about every PR feature no matter how big or small it is. You never know who's watching/reading and it could lead to more PR.
- Mention on your tutoring profiles (*like tutormatch.com or tutorprofiles.com*) that you've been featured in the media. For instance, one of my profiles says that I've been featured in *The Guardian* (a big UK newspaper) and when potential clients see that they're usually so impressed that they don't bat an eyelid at the fee I charge. They just automatically think I'm great at what I do and will pay for the best.
- Post it on all of your social media accounts including LinkedIn.
- Feature logos (of the places that have featured you) on your website.

For example:

The minute a potential client sees logos on your website's homepage (the front page of your site), they automatically associate you with being good at what you do. You're so good in fact that other places (like magazines, newspapers, blogs, radio shows) have started to notice and have mentioned/featured you as a result.

Becoming a high-paid tutor is about showing potential clients that you're the best in your field, what better way to do that than through PR?

Your homework:

1. What type of publications would you like your tutoring business to be mentioned/featured in?
2. Write down whether you'd like them to be in magazines, on the radio, in newspapers, blogs or a combination of all of them.

3. Research **12 media outlets** (including radio stations and blogs if you chose those) that you'd like to be featured in over the next 12 months. **Write their names down**.
4. Head over to their websites and try to find contact names and emails for each of them. If you struggle to find any, simply try to find a contact number and then call the outlet and ask for the email of the person you're looking for. For example, if you're looking for the features editor, ask for the email address of that editor.

Final Thoughts

In this digital age, it's imperative that you familiarise yourself with online marketing methods as they can cost-effectively help you to start, grow and build a tutoring business without you having to spend thousands on upfront marketing and advertising expenses.

We're lucky to live in an era whereby it's possible to make a decision to become a tutor, create free social media pages to promote our services and then receiving enquiries from potential clients without the hassle of getting a loan to pay for a brick and mortar store or office. I think it's vital that we use this to our advantage as tutors and education professionals.

If you love teaching and you truly believe that you have a special gift and ability to inspire, educate and motivate through your tuition lessons then you should make the most of the marketing channels that are available to you. Remember, when you market your business, you're getting your services in front of the very people that need your services the most. You're making an impact and a difference in the lives of dozens of people. Tutoring is truly a remarkable job and we, as tutors should be honored to be a part of this industry. The fact that it's set to grow means that there's even more scope to make as big an impact as possible and help to transform other people's lives through our tuition lessons and skills.

If you're new to tutoring and you're not sure how to start your business or get online tutoring clients, my best tip is to follow the steps and strategies I've outlined in this book. Make sure all of your social media profiles have your email address and contact number (have a separate number for business enquiries) so that people can contact you even if you don't yet have a website. This will allow you to generate leads, prospects and new clients without spending any money on an expensive website or learning how to build a site yourself.

If you're an experienced tutor, use the advice in this book to make tweaks to your existing marketing efforts. Reach out to magazine editors and bloggers, get involved in social media groups and pay attention to where your target market is hanging out online. In doing so you'll build your business without spending thousands on advertising and marketing costs.

I hope you've learnt something new as a result of reading this book. If you'd like to receive additional help to help you with building your tutoring business, download my free step-by-step guide to online marketing. Click here to get it.

Click here to get your copy.

Made in the USA
Coppell, TX
05 September 2020

35682595R00022